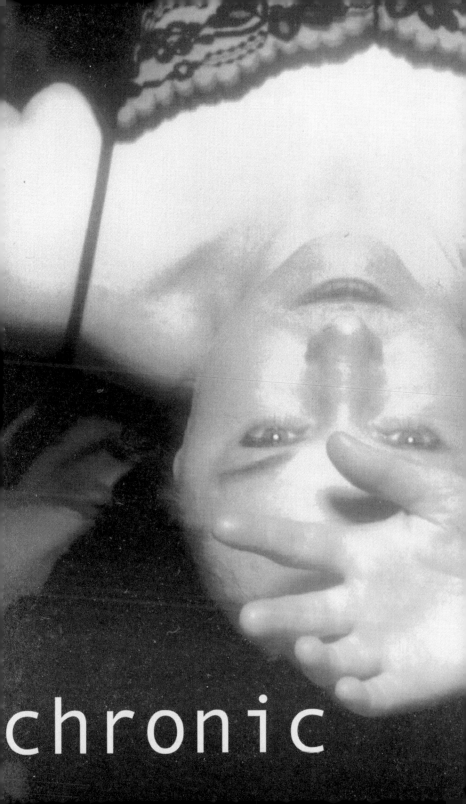

chronic

Chronic

Linda Griffiths

Playwrights Canada Press
Toronto • Canada

Playwrights Canada Press
215 Spadina Avenue, Suite 230, Toronto, Ontario CANADA M5T 2C7
416-703-0013
orders@playwrightscanada.com • www.playwrightscanada.com

Playwrights Canada Press acknowledges the support of
the taxpayers of Canada and the province of Ontario through
The Canada Council for the Arts and the Ontario Arts Council.

Cover photograph of Caroline Gillis by Nir Bareket.
Production editing/cover design: JLArt

Library and Archives Canada Cataloguing in Publication

Griffiths, Linda, 1956-
    Chronic / Linda Griffiths.

A play.
ISBN 0-88754-666-8

    I. Title.

PS8563.R536C47 2004   C812'.54   C2004-904056-1

First edition: July 2004.
Printed and bound by AGMV at Quebec, Canada.

to all those with mysterious illnesses... everywhere...

Alien Creatures and the Ecology of Illness: Linda Griffiths' *Chronic*
by Jerry Wasserman

In the age of AIDS and SARS, mad cow, West Nile and avian flu, when the very staffs of life—sex and food and the air we breathe—can kill us, along comes Linda Griffiths' latest play. Ostensibly about CFS (chronic fatigue syndrome) and the virus that may or may not cause it, *Chronic* puts one woman's *dis-ease* under the theatrical microscope along with various other pathologies of modern life. At first Petra seems familiarly neurotic, a Woody Allen character refracted through George F. Walker. But as Griffiths examines the psychological, social and sexual dimensions of Petra's experience in her desperate pursuit of a cure, as well as her medical treatments, her strange dreams, and the peculiarities of her post-industrial workplace, the stage becomes an environmental petrie dish, a fascinating experiment in the ecology of illness.

Petra works as a web designer at Dynergy Mobilities. "We're riding the wave of a new connectivity," boasts her boss, Oscar. But Petra's design for living has failed her. The intricate webs connecting all the facets of her life to each other and to other organisms have overwhelmed her. The wave has broken and she struggles to keep from drowning. To stay afloat she hangs onto the rational notion of a virus. After all, if a virus can paralyse elaborate computer systems then surely it can explain her own creeping paralysis. But five years of tests and every conceivable therapy have not even produced a successful diagnosis, so she has turned to Diane, a doctor who has "gone outside the boundaries of allopathic medicine" to specialise in alternative therapies and the subconscious roots of illness. Diane's psychosocial explanations often sound simplistic: "Happy people don't get sick." But Griffiths refuses the easy satire this kind of target invites. Diane has her own doubts about the medical strategies that she has chosen and that Petra adamantly resists. Eventually though, the visualisation exercise she prescribes ("imagine that you're walking in a forest") comes to inform Petra's most illuminating dream. And the reversion therapy Diane attempts, involving Petra's primal memory of her parents, yields potentially valuable results.

Another of Petra's life-preservers is her boyfriend and co-worker, Chris. Like so many of the husbands and lovers in Griffiths' plays, he is the best of men and the worst of men: patient with Petra and supportive, passionate and encouraging, two-timing and treacherous. He has his own theories about environmental catastrophes and failing immune systems that involve the Pentagon and the CIA. Though Chris hangs in there and seems like a pretty good guy overall, he ultimately reminds me of those men in "Sex and the City" who finally just aren't enough for the women. Petra needs something more to bring her life back into balance and strengthen her own immunities. She has no circle of girlfriends nor systems of family support so it doesn't seem completely strange that she should find herself drawn to other women – except that those women *are* strange. Amber, the receptionist at Dynergy, like Chris, is both more and less than she seems. A sexed-up bubblehead who is after Petra's job, she develops surprising empathy for her rival and becomes another key element in the complex symbioses that comprise Petra's life.

Petra's primary relationship is with the Virus, the smoothest, funniest, smartest, nastiest, sexiest, scariest character in the play. Her obsession with her illness, her hyper-consciousness of her body and its symptoms, has turned Petra essentially inward. The quality time she spends with the Virus may just be a function of this narcissistic self-obsession: a dialogue with herself. "I'm supposed to fall in love with myself," she tells Diane, "that's what all the wellness books say." But if the Virus is just a figment of her imagination or an expression of her fragmented ego, he's a terrifically vivid one. As written, and as played in the original production by the protean Eric Peterson, the Virus has the strongest presence in Petra's life. He guarantees her friends, offers her love, and gives her better sex than Chris does. He's philosophical ("illness can't help being a metaphor") and oh so eloquent when describing why he's irresistible: "…your affirmations, your visualisations, your teen images are like a pinky finger in a contaminated dike, holding back a sea of little blind beasts with open mouths, yakking to each other, telling the cell to produce thousands, millions of new intruders…. Love me. Accept me. That's all I want." Sharing a body, they have an intimacy that cannot be denied.

Eric Peterson and Linda Griffiths had shared a body before, in a manner of speaking, back in her early Theatre Passe Muraille days. When Griffiths took her mega-hit *Maggie & Pierre* to New York in 1980, Peterson played the third character, Henry the reporter, whom Griffiths herself had portrayed along with the two Trudeaus in her original one-woman show. Peterson also starred in John Gray's *Health: The Musical* (1989) as a character something like *Chronic*'s Petra. Obsessed with his own articulate physiology, Gray's anxiety-ridden Mort has a body that reminds him of his poor health in three-part harmony sung by actors representing his anal, oral and genital regions. This staging of a character's interior dialogue, in which the interior is embodied by a second (or third or fourth) actor, has an even earlier precedent in Canadian theatre. Robertson Davies' 1948 one-act comedy *Eros at Breakfast*, subtitled "A Psychosomatic Interlude," pits a young man's Intelligence against his Solar Plexus as he writes poetry and woos a young lady, accompanied by a chorus of Heart and Liver.

The immediate sources of *Chronic* can be found in Griffiths' own work. Virus, like the title character of Griffiths' 1999 solo portrait of poet Gwendolyn MacEwen, is an alien creature. Both speak directly to their audience, their first lines an ironic echo. "You're so beautiful," begins Gwendolyn. "God, I'm so beautiful," exclaims Virus. Petra is possessed by her virus, Gwendolyn by the creative-destructive power of her poetry. I don't want to push these parallels too hard; the plays are fundamentally different. But an audience or reader familiar with *Alien Creature* and the rest of Linda Griffiths' theatrical canon will not find *Chronic* unfamiliar. Along with the virtuoso writing that characterises all her plays appear certain common structural and thematic qualities.

For one thing, her central figure is almost always a woman engaged in a struggle for power. (*O.D. on Paradise* [1982] and *Brother Andre's Heart* [1993] are the exceptions, both driven, in Griffiths' words, by "multiple characters searching for transcendence.") Think of Maggie Trudeau. Or Wallis Simpson in *The Duchess* (1998). Or *Jessica* (1981), the story of a Métis woman fighting to realise her power and come into her own possession. The pregnant character SHE in *The Darling Family* (1991), like Petra, is thrown into crisis by something living inside her, and she battles her mate to determine whether she alone should have the power to abort or not. Almost every play features some kind of "alien" invasion or visitation. (*Alien Creature* is subtitled "a visitation from Gwendolyn MacEwen.") Maggie and Wallis are themselves alien invaders in their plays, violating and outraging the Canadian and British ruling classes. And Griffiths' female protagonist is always wrestling with or channelling the power of some other dimension. Petra's rich dream life and the microbiological world that the Virus inhabits in *Chronic* are part of a submerged reality of body, spirit or imagination of which all the Griffiths women partake: from Maggie, "a true daughter of the Age of Aquarius" with her visions of people dancing naked in the woods, to the Gods and Amazons and "magic women" from whom Gwendolyn draws her power. SHE throws the I Ching and practices past-life regression; Blue Jays fan Pamela in *A Game of Inches* (1992) channels crazy slugger George Bell in her Toronto living room. Jessica goes "to the dark side" where she confronts the fierce animal spirits of Bear, Coyote and Wolverine; Wallis visits the mock-brilliant looking-glass world of Faerie, full of foppish aristocrats and dancing jewels. Some of these women are desperate, some desperately funny. Usually they are both.

In *Chronic* Linda Griffiths has written what she calls an "ecodrama," tracing the multitudinous connections and delicate balances linking the seen and unseen, the present and past, the psychological, physiological, technological and just plain illogical. Petra is a classic Griffiths female caught up in the apocalyptic twenty-first century where new diseases spawn, for which there are no cures, and overburdened systems fail. But unlike *Oryx and Crake*, Margaret Atwood's dystopian fantasy of ecological despair, *Chronic* doesn't show us a wasteland ravaged by fatal plagues and self-inflicted poisons. Not yet. Just a girl who can't get better and a wisecracking virus and a coupla martoonies after work. Enjoy the show. And try not to catch anything.

———————

Jerry Wasserman is an actor, critic, and Professor of English and Theatre at the University of British Columbia. Editor of Modern Canadian Plays, now in its 4th edition, Jerry has published widely on Canadian theatre, performed on most of Vancouver's stages, and has more than 200 credits in TV and film. His theatre reviews can be heard on CBC radio and read on www.vancouverplays.com.

Chronic premiered at Factory Lab, Toronto, produced by Factory Lab in association with Duchess Productions, in January, 2003 with the following company:

Petra	Caroline Gillis
Diane	Brooke Johnson
Amber	Holly Lewis
Chris	J.D. Nicholsen
Virus	Eric Peterson
Oscar	Graeme Somerville

Director: Simon Heath
Creative Consultants: Sandra Balcovske, Leah Cherniak
Set and Costume Design: David Boechler
Lighting Design: Andrea Lundy
Music and Sound Design: Richard Feren
Stage Manager: Randa Doche
Apprentice Stage Manager: Giselle Clarke
Head of Props: Lisa B. Ryder, Tracy Taylor
Head of Wardrobe: Erika Connor
Cutter: Ina Kerklaan
Scenic Artist: Lisa Laratta
Set Install Crew/Electricians: Duncan Morgan, Seah Gogarty,
   Mathew Ward, Chris Carlton
Scenic Carpenters: Drew Asleep, Duncan Morgan
Graphic Design: Karen Munro, Amy Spring, KD Design
Photography: Nir Bareket
Printing: The Incredible Printing Company
Production Thanks: Nathaniel Kennedy, Tarragon Theatre, Lorraine Kimsa Theatre for Young People, Brad Archdeakin

Chronic was commissioned by Factory Theatre in association with Duchess Productions. Duchess Productions, in association with Factory Theatre, developed *Chronic* through a series of workshops. We wish to thank the following list of remarkable actors who participated in the development of this play: Bruce Beaton, Nancy Beatty, John Blackwood, Colombe Demers, Robert Dodds, Rosemary Dunsmore, David Ferry, Shari Hollett, Maggie Huculak, Randy Hughson, John Jarvis, Jim Jones, James Kidne, Rosa Laborde, Keira Loughran, Chas Lowther, Darren O'Donnell, James O'Reilly, Michelle Pollack, Karen Robinson, Tara Rosling, Booth Savage, Waneta Storms, Dragana Varagic.

characters

PETRA   36 years old. A web designer for a small dot com company, Dynergy Mobilities

CHRIS   36 years old. Petra's boyfriend, a programmer with Dynergy Mobilities.

AMBER   22 years old. Receptionist at Dynergy Mobilities.

OSCAR   30 years old. The owner of Dynergy Mobilities

DIANE   40 years old. A medical doctor experimenting with non traditional remedies.

VIRUS   Millions of years old. The virus that may or may not cause a myriad of chronic diseases.

playwright's notes

Most people are afraid of illness, but in this play, no one is. Instead, they're perverted, instead the virus pulls them in, makes them stick to the illness (and each other) like glue. They all want to run, but they all end up kissing each other instead. As they kiss they spread it, if that is how it's spread, if the virus exists, and if it causes anything. Viruses just want to exist, like anybody, and they like company. They are compulsive communicators, that's why they like computers so much. "It is the age of the virus," meaning things propagate quickly now, they can spread with the touch of a key. We love our viruses, it's just so hard to say goodbye, and they never listen, do they? Only in nature, inner and outer, is there some balance, only in the inner forest is there light.

It's not an easy play to do. It has to be done simply. Rely on your actors, let them find it. You can't take it literally but you still have to use your mind. The dream is the DNA of the piece. It's emotional, don't be too tasteful.

Thank you for reading it.

special thanks

Paul Thompson, Lucinda Sykes, David Young, Nicki Guadagni, Layne Coleman, Ross Manson, Bruce Griffiths, Kevin Kennedy, Robert Fones, Aphra Zimmerman, Sharon Stearns, Colin Viebrock, Anne Braund, Cathy Bluck, Natsuko Ohama.

chronic

ACT I

clusters

DIANE   They started arriving in clusters. I don't know why this city. Why here and not some other place. After HIV and AIDS, it seemed that the new viruses had been identified, but then it was possible there were strains we knew nothing about. It could have been environmental toxicity or a CIA conspiracy, or they'd all done the same drug in their youth. Such a bizarre concoction of symptoms. Nausea, exhaustion, muscle spasms, metallic tastes in the mouth, mental confusion, blurred vision, skin sensitivities, fevers, rashes – digestive organs swelling and shrinking, sometimes preceded by a tingling sensation. Some complained of visual abnormalities – seeing unusual colours, or bright specks like Christmas tinsel. They were basically untreatable. At first I saw nothing that could be diagnosed, then gradually I started to listen to them, as they wept in my office and my computer began to send strange messages – their strangeness seemed to permeate everything. They never seemed to get better, and they didn't seem to die. If it was caused by an organism, then where was it? We couldn't see it. *(to audience)* How are you feeling? How's the digestion? Any other symptoms? Not that it's inevitable. One of the many symptoms is anxiety. Whatever this is, it isn't life-threatening unless you count the suicides. There's no reason to assume anything will happen to you. Still, it's best to be prepared. I want you to know that there are doctors and nurses standing ready in the back of this auditorium should you have the need. Should you need to scream.

the examination

PETRA   I've had needles in my eyelids, fingers inside my anus, I've had cranial therapy, visceral therapy, play therapy, I've had my urine analysed, my saliva analysed, my feet punctured,

I've been submerged in a tank, I've watched my own shit pass by me in a tube, I've had bear grease rubbed on my back by Native healers, I've been hooked up to electrodes, I've cried in the streets. You don't think there's anything wrong with me.

DOCTOR   I think there's a lot wrong with you.

PETRA   You mean emotionally? Of course. Emotions are so convenient, if a doctor can't help you, they always say "it's emotional." And by the time they say that, you're a raving maniac, so of course it's emotional.

DIANE   And this started five years ago?

PETRA   About five jears. Shit, my brain's gone. Sometimes I slur my words. Five *years*, maybe longer. Five years.

DIANE   Were there any special pressures in your life when this started?

PETRA   Don't go there. I mean it. I'm a person, things go bong, wrong–
You see? Like I've drunk too many martinis. It's especially bad around *home* and *bathroom*.

DIANE   Stress?

PETRA   Stress is just a buzz-word they made up so no one would notice what's happening.

DIANE   Who are "they"?

PETRA   You said you understood, back then you said something, I can't remember… I can't sit like this any more.

DIANE   Tired?

PETRA   Pain.

DIANE   And you're how old?

PETRA   I don't remember, I keep lying. I'm thirty-six. Or seven.

DIANE   And what do you do?

PETRA   I'm a web designer, but since this happened I mostly do lowly programming. I work, used to work with a small dot-com company.

DIANE   Computers?

PETRA   Yes. Computers. My boyfriend and I both work there…
used to work… I don't know if I can do this.

DIANE   You're in a relationship? Is it long term?

PETRA   I can't tell you how sick I am. I have Chronic Fatigue
Syndrome – the real thing. Or CFS, it sounds better as an
acronym. That's all I want to talk about.

DIANE   I need to ask these questions.

PETRA   No you don't. It's the disease of a thousand names, but it
has no name. I'm classic, chronic, it's devastated my life.
Can you help? Do you have a plan? You were the next on
the list. I'm sorry if I'm not polite. I lost polite.

DIANE   There is a profile that goes with these symptoms, a majority
of women with driven personalities…

PETRA   It's a virus. The CFS virus. It's the age of the virus.

DIANE   We all carry viruses, they're part of our natural physiology.
Eighty percent of the world's population carries the Epstein
Barr virus. With CFS there is no evidence of any virus at all.

PETRA   People are working twelve-hour days just to stay in the loop
and you have to go home after four hours and spend the
whole next day in bed and the regular medical people can't
do anything and the alternate people say they can but
they're liars and you start to have this relationship with
whatever health practitioner they want you to get better
and you don't and they get angry or stupidly optimistic and
then you go to the next doctor and the next and you realise
you're chronic and you're fucked.

DIANE   How sick are you? On a scale of one to ten. If ten is the
sickest you've ever felt and zero is fine, what number
would you rate right now? Come on, I'm tired, you're
tired, everybody's tired. It doesn't mean you're sick.

PETRA   No. I can't do this. I can't answer one more doctor's fucking
questions and you're going to want to get inside my head
and I don't want you inside my head. *(stands up on bed)*
Owwwww! My knee, it does that. So does the other one.

Sorry. *(looks up to heaven)* Thank you. Thank you for testing me in this way. *(to DIANE)* And thank you.

DIANE   One to ten. Your emotional life.

PETRA   What's ten? Suicide?

DIANE   I have to tell you, I don't believe CFS is a – for lack of a better word a "genuine" illness.

PETRA   That's because it has a stupid name. How can you take *Chronic Fatigue Syndrome* seriously? Everybody's tired, you said it. Everybody's body hurts. It needs a snazzy bio-tech name. Creutzfield-Jakob Disease, but I think that's taken.

DIANE   We think of a burst appendix as physical and depression as not physical, but if you thought of trapped emotions as a web of energy that could hurt you as much as guns or bombs, you might start to make a shift.

PETRA   I thought you were a regular MD who also did alternate therapies so you'd be covered.

DIANE   Not the remedies and not the extra time I would spend with you.

PETRA   A whole sub-culture is making money off the sick.

DIANE   I also have to let you know that I'm being investigated by the medical association. In the last few years, in order to treat patients like you, I've gone outside the boundaries of allopathic medicine. I prescribe vitamins and herbs, and I work with subconscious roots of illness.

PETRA   I told you, I've been there with the emotions. It's a virus and it doesn't care if I'm happy or sad.

DIANE   I would want to know your dreams, the thickness of your saliva, the rhythm of your breath, how your mind works, what your blood smells like. And I would like to hypnotise you. Lie down.

PETRA   I've been to weirder people than you.

DIANE   I'm going to touch your lower belly, tell me if that's not okay.

PETRA   Wow, that's kind of sexy.

DIANE	As I tune into you, the boundaries between patient and doctor can be lost. I try to fight it as / much as I can.
PETRA	/ But you have to promise…
DIANE	What?
PETRA	Promise that you'll…
DIANE	What? Promise what?
PETRA	That you won't give up on me. Sometimes when you don't get better, they give up and… I swore I wouldn't cry.
DIANE	I won't give up on you. *(continuing to touch PETRA's lower belly)*
PETRA	Do you want to kiss me?
DIANE	Kiss you?
PETRA	Yes.
DIANE	No. Are you always this narcissistic?
PETRA	I'm supposed to fall in love with myself, that's what all the wellness books say. And you did want to.
DIANE	I'd like you to imagine that you're walking in a forest.
PETRA	No, not the forest thing. It's not relaxing, I hate forests.
DIANE	Think about what it was like when you first started to feel these symptoms. Close your eyes, I'm going to count backwards from ten. Ten. See a forest, the one you dreamed of when you were twelve years old. Nine. As you walk down the path, your muscles melt away from your feet. Breathe, step, wait. Eight. Begin to notice details, the trees are twisted and overgrown, vines strangle each other, tent caterpillars drop in your hair. Seven. Seedlings are growing out of rotting tree trunks, the colour of green so sweet it breaks your heart. Think of your heart. Six. Begin to hear the sounds of the forest, breathing and eating and killing. Five. Come to a small pool, the surface is covered with slime. Four. See the slime as pregnant, full of possibility. Three. It's raining, the raindrops become lead balls as they smash into the pool. Two. The surface starts to bubble and seethe. One. Where are you?

the fight

PETRA	That's not true!
CHRIS	I don't care what you say… YOU'RE AFRAID OF ME.
PETRA	I'm not.
CHRIS	I'm not an ogre.
PETRA	Because you're a man. Okay, I'm afraid of men.
CHRIS	Not good enough.
PETRA	Because I want you to do what you're doing to me, and I'm afraid of it too.
CHRIS	What do you think I'm doing to you?
PETRA	Make me real. Make me fight like real people fight, make me feel real.
CHRIS	I can't make you real.
PETRA	Yes you can. You'll attack me and make me work hard, attack my bullshit, my phonyness.
CHRIS	You want me to kill you, is that it?
PETRA	Maybe.
CHRIS	Last night, when we were going over and over that thing again, I wanted to strangle you in your sleep, doesn't that bother you?
PETRA	No.
CHRIS	That's sick.
PETRA	It's love.
CHRIS	I don't want to be your father or your therapist. This is bad for me, it's bad for you, just let me go.
PETRA	I'd see us both dead first.
CHRIS	Can you hear yourself?
PETRA	Why do I have to *let* you go? Why can't you just go? Because for the first time in your "polyamarous" life, you've found somebody stronger than you.

CHRIS	Tougher than me.
PETRA	I am not letting you leave me.
CHRIS	How are you going to stop me?
PETRA	Just watch me.
CHRIS	How?
PETRA	Do the thing about my eyes. Come on, be romantic for a second. The part about spring green?
CHRIS	Why?
PETRA	I used to see leaves in your eyes. Green spring leaves, and a small clear pool, and the branches would lean over and…
CHRIS	Drop tiny drops of rain in the pool.
PETRA	You see?
CHRIS	Now I look in your eyes and I see Netscape navigators. You're disappearing up the ass of a computer tube.

CHRIS leaves.

PETRA	*(crying)* You can't say you don't love me. You can't say that.

i'm so beautiful

VIRUS	God, I'm so beautiful. They don't think you're real, you're so good-looking they think you're an *objet*, I'm here to say I am not an *objet*. I've lived longer than they think, inhabiting a shadowy borderline between life and death in the eleven dimensions of the subatomic world. Then there's the ancestral quality of the primeval ooze, the replicant, the compulsive communicator, exchanging the pluripotent code of life like nasty gossip over an over-priced cafe latte. I am slime. I'm yours forever. I like you. You're such a loser. You've been fighting with your boyfriend again, he doesn't see the real you. *(singing)* It's martoonie time, it's martoonie time… just a little retro thing. The body forgets nothing. This girl. Every night, when her father came home from work, like the minute he walked in the door, her

mother would greet him with a martini. "Darling, make it so dry I'll be puckered forever." They would sit and discuss the day. Then they'd have the second martini. The second martini was dangerous, too bright. The father began to turn on the mother. The body forgets nothing. The intruder attaches itself to a cell, the cell wall opens to try and destroy it and that is its fatal mistake, the intruder is now inside, it reprograms the cell's own DNA and starts issuing new orders. Union, transcription, replication, assembly, release. Talking to you is like talking to myself. I love your clothes, where did you get them? I'd like to meet you again. I just want to stake my claim. Feeling a little tired? "Stressed" as they say? How's work? Scream. Scream. Get it out. You'll have to eventually. You're such a perfect specimen. Scream. You'll thank me. Come here, come closer, baby. Sometimes a scream is a kiss, and a kiss is a scream.

>   *They scream / kiss.*

See you later, incubator.

dr. chris

>   *PETRA and CHRIS are sleeping. PETRA wakes up gasping.*

CHRIS   What! What is it?

PETRA   *(trying to breathe)* I can't… I can't…

CHRIS   You were dreaming. You're awake now. Here, sit up.

PETRA   It was sitting on my chest. Like a snowflake Christmas ornament but with long animal teeth and it bit my bum and took out a whole chunk of my cellulite.

CHRIS   I'll bite your cellulite arrghhhhh…

PETRA   No, I still can't breathe.

CHRIS   Do you want some water?

PETRA   I don't know. Maybe… ahhhhhh…

CHRIS	What?
PETRA	I must have pulled a muscle or something.
CHRIS	Let me rub your back.
PETRA	Okay…
CHRIS	Are you sure?
PETRA	No.
CHRIS	There's no way to know where you are with you. The only time I don't feel left out in the cold is when we have sex.
PETRA	That's not what the fight was about.
CHRIS	You don't want me. You like the idea of me.
PETRA	Why do you stay if you don't want to?
CHRIS	I'm here under protest. I don't want to be with you, but you won't let me go, and I will stay until you're honest enough to say, "I don't want you."
PETRA	You've stayed for a whole six months, you're probably my mate for life.
CHRIS	Is that what you want?

Becoming sexual.

PETRA	Not now.
CHRIS	Don't insult me. I know "not now." And six months for me is close to a world record.
PETRA	You like the pain.
CHRIS	Maybe.
PETRA	My whole body's starting to ache.
CHRIS	You're not going to die. Dr. Chris says so.
PETRA	But Dr. Chris has had a lot of patients. All women.
CHRIS	And they're all still alive.
PETRA	I feel so sick.
CHRIS	Come here.

PETRA	You're good at this, I never would have known.
CHRIS	My mother had migraines, I used to soothe her to sleep.
PETRA	I'm sorry about criticising you at work.
CHRIS	You do it again, I'll break your neck.
PETRA	Okay.
CHRIS	Feeling better?
PETRA	I have no more ideas, I haven't had a new idea for a design in six years, I'm recycling myself and I'm starting to sink. I used to dig down for images and they came welling up from somewhere….
CHRIS	Go to sleep.
PETRA	I see little tinsel things in front of my eyes.
CHRIS	And I warned you, right?
PETRA	Whatever that means.
CHRIS	Don't trust me.
PETRA	I don't.
CHRIS	Sleep tight.
PETRA	What were you like when you were twelve years old?
CHRIS	I was a total hero.
PETRA	You love me like the twelve-year-old you were.
CHRIS	Very good.
PETRA	All of a sudden you're so nice. Why?

dynergy mobilities

OSCAR	Whatever time you need, just take it. Take two, even three days. God knows I have a bad back, the pain, I can't tell you. Acupuncture, let me give you the number, all you need is a few needles, and you're out in fifteen minutes.

AMBER	Then there's visceral work, have you heard of that? They use energy and they manipulate your organs. It could be your lymph glands, or your intestines, it's probably for sure your liver, and don't eat yeast, or you'll become one big pulsing blob of candida. *(phone rings)* Dynergy Mobilities? Oscar? Line one.
OSCAR	And you should be seeing a homeopath. Somebody must know one. The royal family uses a homeopath and look at them, they live forever. *(phone)* Yes?
AMBER	Oscar?
OSCAR	*(the phone)* It's dead.
AMBER	Line two.
CHRIS	No, I've got it. Dynergy Mobilities? Yes we can. We'll e you our templates... no problem...
OSCAR	Take care of yourself, Dynergy Mobilities needs you. We're riding the wave of a new connectivity, we don't know the repercussions of the torrents of data spilling into the global consciousness, we only know we're riding the wave. There are hundreds of thousands of start-up companies out there, how are we different? Because of our strategising, because of our team. In two years there will be unprecedented growth, everyone will have e-mail, hundreds of millions of people will be on the web. The old function of design was to fashion the image of a specified outcome, now it's been displaced by the pressing need to articulate the ends themselves. There isn't one answer to a problem, there is a synergistic multiplicity of answers. And so, I ask you all to commit even more fully to Dynergy Mobilities, not because of your own self-interest, but because of the connectivity of the dream.
CHRIS	Well done Oscar, just remember the other goal, wealth acquisition. Let's keep that as part of the dream.
PETRA	I shouldn't be here anyway, it's too distracting. I'll work at, what's it called... the place you go... uh, you know... something is where the heart is... bome... bong. Hong. Hobe.

AMBER	Petra, don't you have to lie down or something?
PETRA	Don't you have to go to college or something?
OSCAR	I'm getting sore just hearing about the whole thing.
AMBER	Me too, and I'm too young to get backaches.
PETRA	So am I.
AMBER	Thirty-one? That kind of thing starts around your age. *(phone)* Dynergy Mobilities. Chris?
CHRIS	Okay. *(on phone)* Could you hold a minute? *(to PETRA)* How are you getting home?
PETRA	I'll just take a cab.
OSCAR	Go home. We'll live. Keep working on those nifty triangles.
PETRA	What?
OSCAR	That idea you were recycling for Retell.
AMBER	But what if what Petra has is catching?
OSCAR	Growth is catching. The matrix of growth is catching… the password doesn't work. Why won't the password…
PETRA	Let me see.
OSCAR	No, no, what's happening? Password invalid…
CHRIS	Everything's shutting down. I just opened my e-mail, and it's gone berserk.
OSCAR	The screen is breaking up into little pieces. Now it's frozen.
AMBER	I'm fine, / no I'm not.
OSCAR	No, no, no. / Stop it. Petra?
AMBER	Something's coming up, it says "Trojan horse." / What's a…
OSCAR	Mine says, "Zombie." We're losing all our files, the corporate lists, the investment profiles, I can't access the back-up…
CHRIS	Something is spreading malicious code, it's infecting the whole system.
OSCAR	Something? What? Like what?
CHRIS	I don't know, like a virus.

the party

PETRA The whole screen is breathing in and out, feet walking, caterpillars dropping, slime splashing, linking into dragon-fly wings opening into... big... triangles.

AMBER enters with a beautifully wrapped gift bag.

AMBER I just thought I'd drop by and see how you were doing. God, it's been six weeks.

PETRA I'm getting an incredible amount done. It's unbelievable, I've been coding like a maniac. It's great, it's just great.

AMBER I thought your computer was broken.

PETRA Frozen. It's fine now.

AMBER So you're not sick, you're just working at home?

PETRA Don't think for a minute that I'm not sick.

AMBER I've never known anyone that's still alive who was out for six weeks.

PETRA My MD says to trust my body and it'll get better by itself.

AMBER I'm not out to get your job or anything.

PETRA You couldn't do my job.

AMBER You don't have to smash that little fact in my face.

PETRA Not smashing, more like mooshing. Nice bag. For me?

AMBER No, for my grandmother. It's wine and some crackers and tapenade from the Italian store and nice soap and... stuff.

PETRA Oh.

AMBER I'm being nice. Because you're sick.

PETRA Oh.

AMBER Like friends? Friendly?

PETRA I've always thought people with lots of friends were kind of gross.

AMBER I have lots of friends.

PETRA	I know.
AMBER	Then you get sick, and people come round. Like when you're a kid and you get all that attention. My sister had asthma, I hated her for it. Would you like me to feel your forehead?
PETRA	Not really.
AMBER	I'm just dying to be a person that feels somebody's / forehead...
PETRA	/ Let's invite some people over. Let's have a party.
AMBER	A party. But you're sick. And you're not exactly...
PETRA	What?
AMBER	A party girl.
PETRA	Unwrap those crackers. *(phones)* Chris? I feel awful. Come over. Bring Oscar too. Bring whoever. Bye.
AMBER	So what have you been doing? Reading a lot, I guess.
PETRA	I've been lying here, watching clouds. When I was twelve years old, I swore that I'd always be the kind of person who watches clouds.
AMBER	Clouds?

CHRIS enters, bringing flowers.

CHRIS	*(to PETRA)* Hi, are you okay?
PETRA	Flowers for me? That's new.
AMBER	Hi.
CHRIS	Hi. *(to PETRA)* I brought you some of that bread somebody said you should eat.
AMBER	You're really getting into this.
PETRA	Sorry for the phone call. I'm a baby.
CHRIS	You're my baby.
PETRA	Am I?
AMBER	We're having a party.

PETRA	When I was a kid and I got sick…

> *DIANE plays PETRA's MOTHER, the VIRUS plays her FATHER.*
>
> *The FATHER has a martini in his hand.*
>
> *They speak in whispers.*

MOTHER	Is her temperature going down?
FATHER	She's still pretty hot. *(thermometer)* Almost one hundred and four.
MOTHER	She's going to go into convulsions. We're taking her to the hospital.
FATHER	Stop worrying.
MOTHER	We should try an alcohol bath.
FATHER	Look, it's only a hundred and three.
MOTHER	We're here, honey. We're just going to wipe you down with a cold cloth. Okay?
PETRA	Don't give up on me.

> *OSCAR enters.*

OSCAR	I've e-ordered tea with no caffeine, crackers with no oil, aspirin with no sugar, milk with no milk, cereal with no wheat, chocolate bars with no chocolate, ice cream with no cream, cigarettes with no tobacco, toothpaste with no paste and beer with no beer. Am I the greatest e-boss that ever lived or what?
AMBER	You're the greatest.
PETRA	Come into my boudoir, make yourself at bong.
OSCAR	What?
PETRA	Make yourself at hog. That's not right, is it?
AMBER	Home. Make yourself at home.
PETRA	Excuse me, I have to go to the kathboom.
OSCAR	The what?
CHRIS	Do you want some help? Let me help you up.

PETRA	It's okay if I move slow.
CHRIS	Just be careful.
PETRA	Thanks sweetie.

PETRA appears to leave.

AMBER	I thought you guys were breaking up?
CHRIS	Where did you get that idea?
AMBER	You told me.
CHRIS	When?
AMBER	After you had that big fight.
CHRIS	What fight?
OSCAR	We call illness and bad luck to us, that's what this guy on public TV was visioning. It's all in the mind. Except he was bald and you have to wonder why he called that to himself. Fear and stress cause cancer. Well, cancer is guilt.
AMBER	Cancer is repression.
OSCAR	Repression and guilt.
AMBER	And stress.
CHRIS	We're not breaking up.
AMBER	But that time, you said…
CHRIS	She was never very strong.
AMBER	She's always been as strong as a horse. I saw that movie, the "she was never very strong" movie. It had costumes and it was boring. I should try getting sick some time.
CHRIS	What do you mean?
OSCAR	Nothing, Amber didn't mean anything. Pent up ambition will give you migraines, I used to have them, then I started the company and they were gone.
AMBER	Maybe men like it when you're suffering from some mysterious illness.
CHRIS	Are you saying she's faking?

AMBER	I'm saying being sick has its advantages.
OSCAR	Owww. Look at that, my lower back's starting to go.
CHRIS	Oscar, what if she's off for a while? Can you hold her job?
OSCAR	Give her another week and she'll be good as new.
CHRIS	But what if it's, like, a couple of months more, can you hold…
OSCAR	I don't know.

PETRA appears to re-enter.

CHRIS	How was it?
AMBER	Do you feel faint?
OSCAR	Maybe you're going to faint.
PETRA	I've always wanted to faint.
AMBER	Me too, I used to practice fainting and saying, "she was never very strong."
OSCAR	Here, let me help you. See, I'm getting into it. Maybe we could get a line of nurses – "www.e-nurseoncall.com"
AMBER	Oscar, that's so Tuesday.
OSCAR	Who's calling me Tuesday, I'm a Monday guy all the way.
CHRIS	There you go.
PETRA	There are some advantages to being sick.
AMBER	Don't say that. Touch wood. Throw salt / over your…
OSCAR	*(to AMBER)* But you said she was taking advantage / of being sick.
AMBER	It's one thing for me to say it, and it's another thing for Petra to say it.
OSCAR	There's a tribe in Africa that believes all illness is caused by a curse.
CHRIS	If there really was a tribe in Africa for every time someone says there's a tribe in Africa… there'd be… I don't know.
OSCAR	Okay, okay.

PETRA	So who cursed me?
AMBER	Maybe it's a blessing in disguise.

> *All freeze except AMBER.*

(to the VIRUS) I see you.

VIRUS	You must be telepathic.
AMBER	Totally.
VIRUS	Jealous of Petra?
AMBER	I am not. I'm sexier than her. And younger and I'm going to go farther and besides I'm not a shitty person like you're saying.
VIRUS	You're bringing tears to my eyes. No, I'm serious.
AMBER	Since she's been sick, things seem to go better for her. I mean, she's lies around, she doesn't have to work, Chris has turned into super nurse and she doesn't look bad. Like that Victorian consumptive thing.
VIRUS	Their eyes would shine and their cheeks would flush, then they would puke their guts out. Literally. Not a speck of blood on a handkerchief but whole gobs of lung tissue. But continue…
AMBER	And I keep gaining weight, no, really, I am, and my skin's breaking out, I've got no guy and I mean it's nuts but, maybe you could, you know…
VIRUS	You want me to do a mojo on you.
AMBER	I've seen this look on her face, like in religion when those missionaries would get horrible diseases and they would thank God for allowing them to suffer for him.
VIRUS	Their suffering put them in contact with a great mystery. Come closer to the mystery. Closer than that.

> *The VIRUS begins to scream in AMBER's face. AMBER pulls away.*

AMBER	I don't think I've thought this out very well. I was just thinking about a fainting spell now and then. But then I could also just fake it, couldn't I?

VIRUS	You see, oh dear, I think I misunderstood.
AMBER	You mean I'm sick now?
VIRUS	You may not have the basic personality. No leaves in the eyes, no clouds in the heart, no chip on the shoulder, no martoonie time. But then again, you could be affected and exhibit no symptoms at all. That would make you a carrier. Or things could be dormant for a period of years, then explode suddenly, a piece of bad news wrapped in protein.
AMBER	I feel sick.
VIRUS	I could do what I want with you, you silly little bitch. There'd be no God you could pray to, no friendly hand that would cool your brow, no drug that would take away the pain. And you would say, "why me," and the answer is, "why not me?" Now run, run as fast as you can go.
AMBER	So what are the symptoms, exactly, Petra?
PETRA	Muscle pain, nausea, exhaustion…
CHRIS	You're not sick, Amber.
AMBER	How do you know?
PETRA	Right, who cares?
OSCAR	Well, if this is a real party, we should have martinis.
PETRA	What?
OSCAR	Martinis, they're making a comeback, back from wherever they went. *Wallpaper* has some recipes and in my bag I have / vermouth and…
PETRA	/ Everybody out. Take your stupid presents and go. Tapenade makes me sick and the soap stinks. And that is not the kind of bread I can eat so get it out of here.
CHRIS	What are you doing?
PETRA	EVERYBODY GET OUT.
AMBER	All he said was we should have martinis…
PETRA	Out. Out. Out. / Out.
CHRIS	/ You can't stand everybody being nice, can you?

PETRA   That's right.

AMBER   Oscar just said, we should / have

OSCAR   Of course, you're not allowed to drink / martinis.

PETRA   / Get out and stop reading *Wallpaper*, it's three months behind.

AMBER   She's got lots of energy now.

CHRIS   FINE. We're going.

PETRA   FINE.

> *As they exit…*

AMBER   She's such a cow.

> *PETRA starts throwing up.*

> *The VIRUS is nice to her.*

VIRUS   There, that's not so bad. Is that better?

PETRA   Yes.

VIRUS   It could be fruit, don't eat fruit, you don't know what they've sprayed on it. Anything could be the reason. People. You've overextended yourself. Don't see so many people.

PETRA   Okay.

VIRUS   It's hard being a cyberqueen.

PETRA   Cyberqueens are twelve.

VIRUS   They all want a piece of you.

PETRA   Not Chris.

VIRUS   Of course not Chris. Amber is very impressed with you, she may want to be you. Some people are like that. Attracted to illness, attracted. Others run at the thought of it, you'll see who stays and who runs.

PETRA   Too many people.

VIRUS   Don't think now, just rest and sleep.

PETRA   How long has it been? How long have I been sick?

VIRUS   About a year. Or two. Or three…

PETRA   Two years?

VIRUS   Or three. Not long at all.

_____perverse

DIANE   All medicine is perverse. Some things you can do
something about, some things you can do absolutely
nothing about. Antibiotics save lives, no one who's
anyone has polio anymore. TB is... well, coming back.
The smallpox vaccine was discovered – a young doctor who
treated a milkmaid who had cowpox, lots of milkmaids got
it apparently, it was nasty but not life threatening. As he was
treating her she said something he never forgot, "Now that
I've got the cowpox, I'll never take the smallpox." It was
true, but why? That was the beginning of vaccines. The
idea of consciously infecting patients with a mild form of
a disease could make the immune system rise to fight the
more dangerous virus. They had to believe viruses existed
even though they were invisible. And then finally they saw
one. They may be the oldest things on earth. You can't kill
them, not ever. They mutate and begin again.

_____victims

DIANE   You're not HIV positive. You don't have Lupis, MS, TB,
cancer, arthritis or Alzheimer's. You're not anaemic, or
diabetic. No Lyme disease, Chrone's disease, or irritable
bowel syndrome. No ulcers. No glaucoma, or cataracts,
your spinal reads normal and there are no kidney stones.
Nothing shows up on the tests.

PETRA   Nothing ever shows up on the tests.

DIANE   There's a lot of anger in your liver.

PETRA   You should see the anger in my small intestine.

DIANE   I want you to concentrate on your anger.

PETRA	I've been sick for five years, I could explode right here in this office.
DIANE	Then do it.
PETRA	I'd blow you to pieces.
DIANE	Go ahead.
PETRA	I don't feel like it now.
DIANE	Perverse?
PETRA	No.
DIANE	What have you been learning from the hypnosis?
PETRA	Sick people are always supposed to be learning something. I live and work in a tangible world, I code my ideas into a machine, and if I don't do something stupid, and the machine doesn't screw up – they stay there. But this ugga bugga…
DIANE	There is so much fear in your body, so much panic, of course your immune system has taken a dive and stayed under. It's terrified to come back. What does it for you? Connecting mind and body, what does it for you?
PETRA	What do you mean, like sex?
DIANE	Maybe, sometimes, yes. You could call orgasm a mind / body connection.
PETRA	/ Where's the mind?
DIANE	In the moment before and the moment after.
PETRA	What is it? What is the mind body connection? What the fuck are you all talking about?
DIANE	Ask your body.
PETRA	Oh no, not "ask your body," that guy was three years ago, and he had a beard, a yarmaka and a thick Russian accent.
DIANE	Your body is telling you something, what is it?
PETRA	The "your body is telling you something" was last year and she was a white gal with an eagle feather who took me for four hundred dollars. The mind / body connection is

supposed to mean that my mind can tell my body not to be sick. My mind and my body don't talk ~~have never talked~~ will never talk to each other and neither do anybody else's. It's a hoax to make doctors feel better.

DIANE   What about music, do you feel it then?

PETRA   What? Feel what?

DIANE   That your mind isn't hanging onto your body for dear life. That your mind and body are one thing, that they're not in conflict, not separate, not compartmentalised. It could be during sex or listening to a poem or just sitting in the sun and relaxing.

PETRA   I have a virus.

DIANE   Fuck you.

PETRA   This is becoming an abusive relationship.

DIANE   Compared to what? You've been placing yourself in the arms of quacks for five years, they abused you, I'm trying to help you. Here take some vitamins, weep in your bed, the world is full of people with mysterious illnesses.

PETRA   If it had a name you could treat it.

DIANE   It doesn't matter if you have a virus or not. There's nothing we can do about "it," but we can treat you.

PETRA   Stop saying "we." What about you? Is your body speaking now? I think your body rules you, just like mine is ruling me.

DIANE   I'd rather be ruled by my body than live in a virtual attic in my head.

PETRA   Good. What else makes you mad?

DIANE   People who see themselves as victims make me mad.

PETRA   No, people not getting better makes you mad, and your specialty is chronic illness. Now who's perverse?

DIANE   I help them to see…

PETRA   That it's all their fault.

DIANE   That they have to take responsibility!

PETRA

Are you supposed to take responsibility for cancer? Now there's a name. If I had cancer and thank you God, I'm glad glad I don't, but if I did, it would be the same thing. Some health practitioner would be telling me that if I got rid of my anger and visualised a shark eating my tumour, it could go away. People are lying on their deathbeds hoping to be saved by "Jaws Three." It's witchcraft.

DIANE

Okay it's witchcraft. And I've seen it work. I have seen strange recoveries, inexplicable deaths, we have power in us we don't know. Call on it. Do whatever it is you have to do to get out of this place. Think, remember. What was going on three years ago?

making an effort

PETRA

So, how was your day?

CHRIS

I don't think Oscar sleeps at all. He's there at four-thirty in the morning, driving himself like an animal. He's living on raw nerves and coffee, he's practically had himself surgically wired to the net, and I don't want to live like that. I'm just not enough of a geek. There are geeks out there who'd be dying to get into a start-up in this market, but I just...

PETRA

I didn't mean give me your whole life story.

CHRIS

So. How are you?

PETRA

Have you ever watched your shit pass by you in a tube?

CHRIS

You saw the colonics guy.

PETRA

Most people say they can't stand to watch, but I was glued to the screen. Faecal tissue, long thin tendrils of it, then mousy like things, shit, more shit, then whole globules of what looks like old kleenex... then just ordinary bits of poo.

CHRIS

Do you feel any better?

PETRA

I took something that's really whacking me out, something's overloading... I think it was the berberis root. Or the grapeseed extract. Something for my liver usually helps but I hope it's not that Gemmo DI stuff at thirty-eight ninety-nine a bottle. So that's… what? One hundred and twenty-nine and you need two loads a month, that's how much a week?

CHRIS   That's…

PETRA   And people aren't returning my messages and e-mails. I haven't heard from Rebecca in two months, and Jennine and Sarah, nothing, and Kaliel who said if I needed anything just let him know.

CHRIS   What kind of messages are you leaving?

PETRA   Sick person whiney letters, why wouldn't they want to dash right over here?

CHRIS   Let's get out of here, let's go to a movie, we'll take it slow.

PETRA   Okay, we could have some appetizers at Kalandar and then go to a movie. A Hollywood blockbuster set in Paris with lots of shooting and bare chests.

CHRIS   Let's go downtown.

PETRA   Downtown's too far.

CHRIS   We could take a cab.

PETRA   I can't do those exercises, I pulled another muscle. Maybe I shouldn't. I can't. Fuck.

CHRIS   If you can't, you can't. We'll just stay home, watch TV.

PETRA   But you want to go out.

CHRIS   I don't have to.

PETRA   I just don't know if I can do it.

CHRIS   Then don't.

PETRA   The way to handle this is to say, "I have good days and bad days." So I'm calling it a good day.

CHRIS   Or a good night.

PETRA   Or a good night.

CHRIS   Really?

PETRA	I don't know. Are you getting excited?
CHRIS	I know better.
PETRA	I can see you are.
CHRIS	So?
PETRA	But I don't know if I can.
CHRIS	Fine.
PETRA	Starting to deflate?
CHRIS	A little.
PETRA	But maybe it will be a good night.
CHRIS	Maybe.
PETRA	Are you getting excited again? Yes you are.
CHRIS	You're so full of shit. And the only reason I can take all this shit, is that I know you're in too much pain to have sex, so just relax.
PETRA	You like it that I'm sick.
CHRIS	Most men are afraid of illness.
PETRA	Everybody's afraid of illness.
CHRIS	But to another kind of man, a certain kind of man, there's something sexual about it. Something necessary, something irresistible.
PETRA	Because I'm weak.
CHRIS	But you've got to stop now. If this was about bringing us together, maybe it's done that, we'll see. But now you've got to stop all this before it's too late. Get better, make up your mind to get better.
PETRA	IT DOESN'T WORK LIKE THAT! PEOPLE MAKE UP THEIR MINDS TO LIVE AND DIE ANYWAY ALL THE TIME.
CHRIS	Are you all right?

PETRA   That's such a turn on. When a person has that look on their face and they say, are you all right? Let me do it to you. Are you all right?

CHRIS   It's true, it feels good.

PETRA   I'll do it again. Are you all right? How was that?

CHRIS   That was good.

PETRA   I want to give it back to you, all the concern you've given me, I want to thank you... can you hear it in my voice? Thank you. Now. Are you all right?

CHRIS   Yes.

PETRA   Are you sleeping with Amber?

CHRIS   Not yet.

PETRA   Don't give up on me.

the sex scene

In blackout.

PETRA   No... ugh... that's it, no my legs / won't open like that...

CHRIS   Is that... okay, / like this...

PETRA   Uhh, no, yeah, maybe. Oh, / that's good.

CHRIS   Good? Yeah, tell me it's good.

PETRA   Yes, oh, oh, that's great... just...

CHRIS   What?

PETRA   No, that's good...

The VIRUS' voice is heard.

VIRUS   Can I do it? Like this?

PETRA   Yes, yes do that. Ohhh God, that's good.

CHRIS   And... is that good... no?

PETRA   No, but... yeah. Oh God yes.

VIRUS	What about this, is this good? *(sucking noises)*
CHRIS	Oh, boy, you never used to… oh man… *(sounds of extreme sexual pleasure)*

office gossip

OSCAR	Oh, I know and she's so narcissistic. Everything's a huge problem, as if she's the only one…
CHRIS	She was always like that, even before she got sick…
AMBER	And at the same time, it's like she's lost her edge.
CHRIS	That's not such a bad thing.
AMBER	I guess it's her parents or something.
OSCAR	Remember when she first got sick, and she did that whole thing with the martinis?
CHRIS	Oh, I know. Her mother used to sneak a cocktail at night and her father was shitty to her. Big deal.
OSCAR	So, it's not like she was locked in a closet and burned with cigarette butts.
CHRIS	No. She just had an ordinary childhood.
AMBER	Like anybody.

on your side

PETRA	I need new friends.
VIRUS	Not at all, I'm starting to really like them.
PETRA	Why?
VIRUS	They do feel compassion, they just don't know how to show it.

PETRA   I don't care about them, I'm trying to work. And my laptop keeps turning everything into raw code.

VIRUS   I like the infection that erases the word "I" from everything in your system. That's my cousin.

PETRA   The screen slowly fills with water, a figure is drowning, the drops of water morph in lead balls and batter the person to a pulp.

VIRUS   I just don't think we should be lonely, we should spread ourselves around.

PETRA   But no one likes me.

VIRUS   I can help with that.

PETRA   I'm supposed to be able to think you away. Watch this, I'm thinking good thoughts, positive thoughts…

          Pause.

VIRUS   Try an affirmation.

PETRA   I now choose to rise above my personal problems to recognise the magnificence of my being.

VIRUS   *(shouts and shudders as if dying)* Just kidding. It's all so rational isn't it? All this control. I liked it better when there was God and he was either angry or he wasn't. God punishes with illness, tests with illness, or he raises his hand and it's gone.

PETRA   What did you mean, you could help me?

VIRUS   Maybe I could make them like you. I'm very persuasive.

PETRA   Really?

VIRUS   Something like that.

PETRA   I'm not denying I want attention.

VIRUS   Attraction. Better than attention. They'd be attracted to the two of us. A submicroscopic *coup d'état*.

PETRA   Do it.

VIRUS   I don't know if I can. You have to give something too. Love me.

PETRA	I hate you. I have everything you've done to my life.
VIRUS	And that attitude is doing you no good. Stop trying to kill me, it's exhausting. Think of all the good I do, bringing organisms closer together, reproducing in new mutant forms… I think things are going very well, Dr. Diane is a real find. Now lie back. On a scale of one to ten, how sick do you feel?
PETRA	Eight.
VIRUS	On a scale of one to ten, how much pain are you in?
PETRA	Eight.
VIRUS	Eight, that's not so bad. Try the bubonic plague potion of a tonic of excrement, cooked with mustard, crushed glass, turpentine, poison ivy and an onion. It'll save you money on alternate therapies.
PETRA	They won't believe in you. Why won't they believe in you?
VIRUS	Because illness can't help being a metaphor.

lipstick scene

AMBER	What's that lipstick you're wearing?
PETRA	It's called Slut.
AMBER	Would you mind picking me up a tube of that?
PETRA	You want to wear the same colour as me?
AMBER	Well, it'll look different on me, because I have different colouring.
PETRA	Why do you think its going to look good on you, if it looks good on me and we have different colouring?
AMBER	I don't know. Can we at least try it?
PETRA	No. Oh, sorry, okay. No, let me do it.

PETRA puts the lipstick on AMBER.

AMBER	I think that looks good. Do you mind if I wear the same colour?
PETRA	No. It sounds like you mind.
AMBER	No. Just maybe if you go back you can pick out something more for your age group, more. Well, it might be a little harsh with your skin.
PETRA	You think it looks harsh?
AMBER	No, I think actually it looks quite good, I'm just saying, maybe it's a little bit harsh.
PETRA	Is it harsh or isn't it?
AMBER	No, you should wear it.
PETRA	I don't have any sisters, I think it's left me deprived of some basic instincts.
AMBER	I've fought to the death with my sisters over a leotard. It's just competition.
PETRA	Do you feel competitive with me?
AMBER	I used look to you as someone I might want to be.
PETRA	You'd want to be me?
AMBER	I'd be better at it than you, I mean I'd be better at being you than you are now because you're sick.
PETRA	Good, I don't want female friends because they'll say things like that. This whole friend thing is overrated.
AMBER	I do think, I don't want to end up like Petra.
PETRA	I can't believe this.
AMBER	In a way you were my model.
PETRA	I need a friend.
AMBER	Well, I think you're being really brave.
PETRA	Brave? Why? Why am I brave?
AMBER	What's wrong with / calling you brave?
PETRA	You know what's wrong with it.

AMBER	Don't get mad, I meant it as a compliment.
PETRA	It's not a compliment!
AMBER	What's wrong with br…
PETRA	Brave is you're doing something stupid and not thinking of the consequences, brave is enduring without complaining, brave is saving little children in flaming houses, brave is dead. Boring people are brave, you say brave with a sad lilt to your voice, like at a funeral. You say brave in the past tense.
AMBER	But you do get that look on your face sometimes. Like there was this girl in the congo or somewhere and the missionaries converted her and she got sick and was in horrible, horrible pain. Horrible, horrible pain. And she never complained, she just prayed all the time. And the missionaries were amazed that this little Black girl, who didn't know anything about God till they told her, was like more saintly than anybody, and when she died, flowers grew up from her grave.
PETRA	If I was dying I'd be brave.
AMBER	You'd be awesome if you were dying.

dream

PETRA	I dreamt I was walking through a forest and I came to a glass building. I walk inside and see a huge rock, white grey like old marble and on the rock are carvings. I know they're very old. At first I'm disappointed, it looks like kids have been let loose with magic markers – stick people, snake squiggles. But then it gets darker and where I saw maybe a dozen, now I see thousands, people and animals, one with a head like a balloon and a long long neck, and the head looks like the sun. A face with a mouth wide open in fear or surprise. More and more creatures and pictures, now swimming and dancing and crawling. Then I see the woman. The rock has a fissure like a deep hole – the

middle of her body and between her legs are taken up by
the hole and then the legs stretch out. It was as if the very
middle, the centre, the hole of her had dropped through the
rock, right down to the centre of the earth.


```
dot com bubble
```

OSCAR	They say illness is narcissistic. Narcissus accidentally coded himself into an HX7 laptop. All of him was right there in front of him, lit beautifully from within. He was entranced. He didn't eat, he didn't sleep, he finally starved, still staring at his own flickering image.
PETRA	Are you firing me?
OSCAR	Ten years ago, you were my image of a cyberqueen.
PETRA	Oh my God.
OSCAR	I thought, with her on my team, this company is going to soar like a bird.
PETRA	Is the company soaring like a bird?
OSCAR	No it's limping like a… no it is flying, that's not true, it is flying, but the sky is not exactly iridescent blue.
PETRA	It's got something sticking to its wings, a little slime weighing it down. I got you clients, people came to you because of me.
OSCAR	I need someone who can converge on a twelve-hour day besides me.
PETRA	I can't work twelve hours. I can't work eight hours, but I can do four hours a day. Most days.
OSCAR	Four hours? And then what? Take a nap?
PETRA	More like fall into bed like a dead person with the drool coming out of my mouth.
OSCAR	Cyberspace never sleeps.
PETRA	Aren't you tired, Oscar? Right now, wouldn't you like a nap?

OSCAR	I hate naps.
PETRA	Do you?
OSCAR	Stop. I mean it. What about going on disability?
PETRA	I can't because there's no medical diagnosis.
OSCAR	Because it's emotional?
PETRA	It's a virus. It's the age of the virus.
OSCAR	E-mail has exploded just like I predicted. People are spending four hours a day just doing e-mail and phone messages. Four hours is not a working day.
PETRA	Even if I could get it, disability is nine hundred and forty dollars a month. Can you live on that?
OSCAR	You get some freedom, you become self employed.
PETRA	People never stop, not at night, not at lunch… I can't do that.
OSCAR	Then you can't compete.
PETRA	My new designs are brilliant.
OSCAR	Your new designs are…
PETRA	What? Okay, fire me.
OSCAR	This Gothforest thing, rotting leaves, nests of caterpillars dropping onto the screen… and even if I liked them, flash is out. No one has time to watch pretty pictures before they get to a website, it's gratuitous animation.
PETRA	But I want multilayering, multiplicity. Things aren't one thing.
OSCAR	Says who? The atmosphere is closing down out there. They want fire walls, protection, warnings.
PETRA	And you're going to give them what they want.
OSCAR	They want protection.
PETRA	They need an immune system.
OSCAR	That was last week.

PETRA	Oscar, I don't know how I'm going to live. All these vitamins and remedies cost a fortune, and my health plan doesn't cover any of it.
OSCAR	Petra, I can't.
PETRA	Don't tell me what you can't do. I left a good job to come to you, everybody wanted me.
OSCAR	Things change.
PETRA	I made your company.
OSCAR	I made my company, by working like a dog. I can't keep you on salary any more, but I will be able to offer you contract work.
PETRA	How much?
OSCAR	I can't guarantee anything. Do you think I like doing this?
PETRA	Oscar, you're missing it. Biology is the new technology. The line in the sand is being drawn between the healthy and the sick, and there's just one question – will you be a patient or will you be a stockholder?

crying scene

PETRA tries to pull on shoes. Pulls a muscle.

PETRA Owww.

PETRA tries to change her top. Pulls a muscle.

Awwoh.

PETRA moves forward to reach. Pulls a muscle. Shouts with pain and anger.

OWWWWWWWWWWWWW!

PETRA starts sobbing. She cries with rage and frustration and pain. This is hopeless crying. There is no release. No one comes to help. The crying scene lasts longer than is comfortable.

conspiracies

DIANE   I'm glad the three of us could get together. Chris, you know what I'm doing with Petra's treatment?

CHRIS   I've heard rumours.

DIANE   How far do you want me to go?

CHRIS   What do you mean?

DIANE   To get inside Petra's illness, I have to climb inside her life, I have to know about this relationship.

CHRIS   Go ahead.

DIANE   You're a brave man.

CHRIS   No, I'm curious about what you're up to. And I've been doing some research myself finally. Information is out there for everybody now, that's what the internet did.

DIANE   I know what the internet did.

CHRIS   What Petra has is an auto-immune disease that's part of a hidden epidemic. Maybe that's news to you, I don't know. New bio weapons are spreading virulent forms of God knows what, or Pentagon experiments on African Green Monkeys got out of hand, it's the food, it's the air, it's the water. CFS might be many diseases, appearing in different forms, with a different panoply of symptoms, depending on the host.

DIANE   Depending on the host? Why?

CHRIS   What?

DIANE   Why is it different depending on the host?

CHRIS   The person's biochemistry, their history…

DIANE   Their history? So whatever they're carrying will make things easier or harder on them physically?

CHRIS   Sure but…

DIANE   That's what I'm doing.

CHRIS   Therapy.

DIANE	Right.
CHRIS	Jesus. How much are you charging her?
DIANE	Therapy, everyone starts at four years old, especially politicians.
CHRIS	You can say that in the face of environmental catastrophe?
DIANE	Mother, father, siblings. Mother father siblings. Explore that and see if you don't feel better, no matter what the Pentagon is doing.
CHRIS	And consistent sabotage from the scientific community? AIDS came from a contaminated vaccine given to gay men by scientists, for hepatitis. / In the seventies.
DIANE	Or AIDS was developed by the American military as a covert weapon. And the African green monkeys / were part of the…
CHRIS	In 1969, the CIA got the go-ahead to develop two new bio weapons, one was lethal and the other disabling. The disabling one was better, it could incapacitate whole sections of a population…
DIANE	That would involve isolating crystalline toxins from various bacteria and whether it's possible is still open to speculation…
CHRIS	No, it's not. That's where the Lake Tahoe-Truckee epidemic comes in. A whole town gets chronic fatigue. They test the pathogen on hogs…
DIANE	Do you know the one about the mosquitos?
CHRIS	I don't know that one.
DIANE	Where in the fifties Canada breeds a hundred million infected mosquitoes a month for the Pentagon. In Belleville?
CHRIS	So you're agreeing with me?
DIANE	In life a lot of people are exposed, why do some people get it and others don't?

CHRIS	Illness is random and that's hard for people like you to accept. When you get a cold, you get a cold, whether you hated your father or not.
DIANE	Why do you say "father," most people say mother when they're coming out with a cliché like that.
CHRIS	You're saying there's no virus, you're saying it's my fault she's sick. Sure it's my fault. That's what everyone thinks. Every woman I've ever been with keeps showing up and telling me it's my fault.
DIANE	Happy people don't get sick.
CHRIS	That's ridiculous. Are you happy?
PETRA	No, I'm sick.
DIANE	The immune system fights infectious intruders, happiness increases the immune system.
CHRIS	Laughing at Steve Martin movies is supposed to increase the immune system.
DIANE	All right, that's it for today. I think this is a good beginning. Thank you for coming, Chris.
CHRIS	It's over?

the body forgets nothing

VIRUS	The body forgets nothing. Not a single negative thought, not when you dreamt your own funeral as a child, not any carnage you've ever seen. It's martoonie time, it's martoonie time. The father started saying things at about the second martini. He'd go at the mother and at her and at her, humiliating her. "You're slurring your words. You can't handle two drinks, just have one." For some reason, the mother couldn't say, "piss off." She could only imagine passive resistance. So, with money she'd saved from her housekeeping allowance, she bought her own bottle of gin, her own vermouth, her own jar of olives and she hid the bottles in the pockets of her old fur coat in the hall

cupboard. Just before the father came home, she would mix herself one cocktail, drink it all alone, then wash the glass and put it away. When the father came home, he'd have two martinis, and she would have one. Only the daughter knew. Don't tell your father. Each bad thought lets the intruder in. You're incomparably smug, having a good day, then you think of doing taxes and that throttle of fear comes, your immune system falls. You try not to think that thought and the trying is lying, and that leads to more negative thinking, the negative thoughts gather momentum, your affirmations, your visualisations, your teen images, are like a pinky finger in a contaminated dike, holding back a sea of little blind beasts with open mouths, yakking to each other, telling the cell to produce thousands, millions of new intruders, they're sucking, tearing away bits of the cell's protective membrane, exulting in their own reproduction. Love me. Accept me. That's all I want. To be your co-traveller through life.

PETRA   The body remembers everything? My mother is wearing a turquoise skirt and cool sunglasses, she's driving a blue car with her elbow out the window and the sunlight is in her dark dark hair. My mother is laughing like a girl at something her sister said, she's laughing so hard, her wrinkles are gone and there's no pain, a young girl with wide blue eyes.

    Blackout.

ACT II

day and night

DIANE   They started calling at all times of the day and night. I'd
          finish for the day, go home and start answering messages.
          None of the remedies seemed to hold, I'd prescribe a
          combination of treatments and three days later I'd have to
          change everything. They were mutable, their systems totally
          unstable. They didn't die. They lived and lived, in worse and
          worse shape, begging insurance companies and government
          agencies for money but there was no money for the non
          critical and they were chronic not critical except when
          chronic became critical no one would say. And the
          suicides, not enough to be statistically important. And
          the spontaneous recoveries, one patient got a dog and she
          was fine. Others dragged themselves from treatment to
          treatment, trying everything. Or maybe they weren't trying
          with a full heart and the one with the dog was? The only
          way forward was to assume that those who got better had
          less general undertow, they were lighter, they could dance
          with the virus. So I worked to make them lighter.

all better

PETRA   Chris, come over here. I feel better. I feel good. Good. Like
          normal, only better than normal. That feeling, the bone
          marrow sick feeling, it's gone. It's gone.

CHRIS   How can you be sure?

PETRA   I'm not sure. I only know right now. Waking up free. Oh,
          God. Oh God. It's gone. I feel good. Is that really true? It's
          like a veil coming off my soul, like I was blind and I can see.
          I don't hurt. I'm sore, all right, a little sore but my brain is
          clear, it feels like a burst of light radiating the sky. Look at
          everything. Look at the walls and the window, oh God it's
          sunny, I can think. I have energy. There are so many things
          I want to do. Shhhh. Maybe this is a trick he wants to play

on me. Be very quiet. My body is thrumming, don't you love that word, "thrumming," shhhh maybe he won't be able to tell.

CHRIS   Maybe he's not listening any more.

PETRA   I want to tell jokes. I want to be funny. I've been thinking about sex, how funny is that?

CHRIS   Very funny.

PETRA   Despair is the only sin, and I didn't despair, not really. I was quite brave. And Dr. Diane did help, even if she's not that smart… it's true I can almost be thankful this happened. I probably am a better person.

CHRIS   You probably are.

PETRA   And my work's better, I think.

CHRIS   It's different.

PETRA   I've been thinking about you and me. About how, when my body's working again and I've exercised all the stiffness away, how we'll make love.

CHRIS   You don't want to go too fast now. Maybe you should sit down.

PETRA   I want to take all day, or at least an afternoon. And I want you to use your hands a lot, do all that stuff with your fingers you used to do. And I'll be able to do more things to you when you're doing things to me, be strong and bendable, find angles, that's something I've missed, the angles, you don't know what's possible, and you're not even inside yet.

CHRIS   Absolutely. / But you should…

PETRA   / Maybe I should learn salsa dancing. There's a class just up the street, I saw the sign a long time ago, such a long time ago… when was that?

CHRIS   That would also be great but you have to be careful.

PETRA   Why do you keep saying that? You are so used to this. Sick Petra is like an old shoe, and when there's trouble, she goes to sleep. Do you want to keep me like this? Are you the virus?

CHRIS Yeah, that's right. I'm the virus.

PETRA I want to be able to fling myself around, I want to be so flexible I can fit inside your shoulder blade, I want to arch back like a bow when you make me come I want to be an arrow up your nose.

CHRIS What?

PETRA I want to be an arrow… up your nose.

CHRIS Oh. Well…

PETRA That doesn't make sense, does it? An arrow up your nose.

CHRIS Just lie down for a bit.

PETRA Stop it. I need to enjoy this beautiful day. I'm going to get a lot of things done. I'm going to find out what's happening at the office, I'm going to phone people and have lunch in the sun and drink coffee. I have to find out about that course, I want to read hard books, I want a new lipstick colour. Sweetheart, go out on a hunting expedition and bring back bad things. Chocolate chocolate mousse, something fried and a couple of macburritos with bacon and lots of cheese.

CHRIS Do you need money? How much did that last load of vitamins cost?

PETRA I just put it on one of my cards. Let's not talk about that now.

CHRIS All your cards are maxed out, aren't they?

PETRA There's one left with a tiny bit of room, and now it's filled.

CHRIS Here, let me give you a hundred bucks.

PETRA No, you go buy bad things.

CHRIS You know, you look great. It's amazing. You look so good.

PETRA Come back quick.

CHRIS exits.

VIRUS	How are you doing? Tired? Very tired?
PETRA	I'm fine. That cocktail of remedies must be finally working.
VIRUS	They broke Anne Frank, you know. They broke her.
PETRA	What do you mean, they broke Anne Frank?
VIRUS	Before she died, Anne Frank was broken.
PETRA	No.
VIRUS	The spirit, the essence, the basic vocals that you loved so much in the inspiring diary that you read when you were twelve. There they are, hiding from the Nazis, and Anne's spirit is so strong. She lost it finally, and became unrecognisable.
PETRA	Anne Frank was never broken, no matter what they did to her.
VIRUS	It was disease that got her, something serious. I forget. Something like diphtheria. That and the dysentery worked up to something like Ebola.
PETRA	It killed her, but it didn't break her, breaking is something that happens inside.
VIRUS	You've been watching too many "Star Trek" reruns, start watching wrestling, someone wins and someone loses and they're on top of each other the whole time.
PETRA	I went, I saw the house in Amsterdam, the stairs going up…
VIRUS	Someone who knew her saw her by the fence in the camp.
PETRA	No.
VIRUS	All this woman said was, "I saw Anne just before she died and she was unrecognisable, I looked in her eyes and she was not the Anne Frank I knew. She was broken."
PETRA	Anne Frank unfolded like a rose in the middle of horrors. Anne Frank was valiant, Anne Frank was mighty. Her heart was my heart when I was twelve years old. You made a bad move when you put down Anne Frank.

the pickup

CHRIS	I'm supposed to pick up some stuff. You work late.
DIANE	I'm trying to do research at night. There's no research money for conditions that don't kill you.
CHRIS	You're poisoning her with all this shit. What kind of witches brew is "mercurious solubulis"? None of this is regulated, it could be anything.
DIANE	It's homeopathic, and has been used for thousands of years.
CHRIS	When does this stop, when she discovers she was Queen Nefertiti in some past life? She's been sick for five freaking years.
DIANE	The five-year mark can be a turning point, if she has a chance, it's now. We have to help her see that.
CHRIS	Is it my fault?
DIANE	A bad relationship can be a doorway.
CHRIS	It's not a bad relationship. It's a relationship where one person is in a kind of nether world and the other isn't. How many couples do you know like that? Everybody. There's lots of guys that would've walked out by now, but I stayed. Five years, almost six.
DIANE	Bully for you.
CHRIS	What does that mean?
DIANE	Why do you stay?
CHRIS	Is this what you meant? You have to crawl inside my life as well as hers?
DIANE	I don't know what I meant. I meant I have to be able to smell her when I go to sleep.
CHRIS	She smells as sweet as a baby.
DIANE	Sorry. I keep saying that. Sorry, I never used to say sorry, we're taught that, doctors are taught never to apologise when things don't work.
CHRIS	It must be awful to see sick people all the time.

DIANE	It is. It's awful. You have to put up a force field not to get drawn into it.
CHRIS	Is your force field up now?
DIANE	Your political rant was right, of course. Everything is corruption and contamination. I look at the brown air and I just want to cry.
CHRIS	Don't cry.
DIANE	The medical world is torn in pieces and terrible things are loose and sometimes love can help and sometimes it can't. It's time to… I don't know. Find God. It's as if all the people in the world who are being eaten alive by illness, all the people all over the world in all the dirty little hovels and refugee camps, are begging me to help. People used to die all the time. They would just die of some infection or the flu or something. Now we live. There are drugs and operations but they barely hold back the floodtide of what's coming I'm a necromancer, I might as well use leeches and bleed people, I'm dabbling in the underworld of disease, I set things in motion and then don't know what to do. I know illness comes from underneath, that there are doorways… that there are doorways…
CHRIS	I don't know what you're talking about.
DIANE	I'm sorry.
CHRIS	Are you all right?
DIANE	What?
CHRIS	Are you all right?

They kiss.

What should we be doing for her?

DIANE	I don't know anymore.
CHRIS	That's just doubt.
DIANE	Everybody's sick now, everybody.
CHRIS	I'm not sick.
DIANE	That's right, you're healthy, aren't you? You're so healthy.

the bath

AMBER	I missed you.
PETRA	I missed you too.
AMBER	I'm sorry, I was swamped, for like, a long time and…
PETRA	It's okay. It's just that I've got this rash all over my arms, I'm not supposed to get it wet and I'm starting to stink.
AMBER	I've never bathed anyone before. I mean, when you don't have kids…
PETRA	You should have kids.
AMBER	I'd never fit into anything again. But now they have those new ab machines, you can get a six-pack two months. How's the temperature?
PETRA	Perfect.
AMBER	Does that feel good?
PETRA	You've got a nice touch. I can't lift my arms very high…
AMBER	Just do what you can.
PETRA	Mmmmmmm.
AMBER	There are a lot of people going to these protests. I think maybe I should show up, but then who wants to get pepper sprayed if you don't have to. Besides a friend of mine went to one and said they're just full of young people trying to get laid. There's nothing wrong with that but a person can get sex just by going to the right club. I'm starting to feel a little strange, just a little odd when I get on the computer in the bornings. But I'm fine. Do you want me to do, like, between your legs?
PETRA	If you don't mind.
AMBER	I've never touched a woman between her legs. This is sick.
PETRA	Sick?

AMBER	Sick means good. So this is what all my boyfriends were feeling. (*washing between PETRA's legs*) Do you mind if I keep on doing this?
PETRA	No, it's nice. Do you ever pray?
AMBER	Pray? Not exactly. I used to be really religious but then nobody else was so I stopped.
PETRA	If someone you love is trapped under a burning car their flesh is starting to melt off their bones and they're screaming help me and you can't you cry out "Oh God!" You pick up the telephone and find out someone you love is the kind of sick where you could die, even if you've never been inside a church in your life you say, "oh God."
AMBER	Or you say "Oh, God!" just before you come.
PETRA	Oh God...
AMBER	Really? Should I stop?
PETRA	No... don't stop...; Oh, oh, God!
AMBER	Are you kidding me? That was fast. I didn't know it could happen that fast. I could do that. Are you all right?
PETRA	Yes.
AMBER	Wow. So, what about you, do you pray?
PETRA	Just before I go to sleep, I've started to realise that I whisper in my head, "love me." Maybe that's a prayer.
AMBER	Love me. I mean it. It's my prayer too. Let me stay here. I'll take care of you. I will cook for you, I will clean for you, I will take care of your life. Don't look at me like that, this is a good offer. You think this sickness is terrible, it isn't. It's beautiful. It's made you beautiful.
PETRA	You'd take care of everything?
AMBER	I'd take away all the stuff from your life and help you get better.
PETRA	It sounds really good...
AMBER	So, it's okay?
PETRA	Uhhh... I don't think so...

AMBER	Why? Don't you want me to?
PETRA	I do but, Amber, Oscar is crazy about you.
AMBER	Oscar?
PETRA	Don't run after me. I don't need any more attention. Go after him.

> *AMBER hands the washcloth to the VIRUS. The VIRUS begins washing PETRA.*

VIRUS	It could be so much worse, you must be aware of that. You're going to get something eventually, why not ease into something more serious with me? A tiny touch of what's coming?
PETRA	"Love your body," Diane says that.
VIRUS	I do.

oscar and amber

OSCAR	Have you seen Petra recently? Do you think that new doctor is doing her any good?
AMBER	I think she's a quack and is taking all her money and doing bad things to her head.
OSCAR	Money. I don't know where she gets the money to pay these people. I don't have it. I've never been able to give it away. Sure, sometimes the mail comes in and there's a picture of some pathetic person with big brown eyes and I throw twenty-five dollars on my Master Charge.
AMBER	The fire-wall system is still selling, everybody's so paranoid now.
OSCAR	We have to downsize. We have to exit somebody.
AMBER	I can tighten my belt.
OSCAR	You're a beautiful girl.
AMBER	And I always thought you were very attractive.

OSCAR	Is that true?
AMBER	Yes. It's just that, you're the one with the company and I'm the office girl, it's a class thing.
OSCAR	Beautiful girls can go places, people with big businesses want beautiful girls.
AMBER	You know, Oscar, beautiful doesn't get you *bupkas* anymore. Beautiful can turn against you these days.
OSCAR	I've kept giving Petra consultant work, but I can't keep it up. You're already doing a lot of her work. It's you or Petra. I have to make choices, but I can't. I'm leaving it up to you. Who would you choose?
AMBER	You've been really good to Petra, you know that? Way better than most bosses would have been.
OSCAR	I haven't slept in nights.
AMBER	I think that's so great. Not that you haven't slept but that you're tormented about being a good person.
OSCAR	No, you're wrong, I don't want to be a good person. You want to stay? You should stay. I want to be good to you. It's time for me to be good to you.
AMBER	You're offering me Petra's job?
OSCAR	At a reduced salary.
AMBER	It's what I always wanted, and I'll take more courses and…
OSCAR	Yes?
AMBER	It's no fair.
OSCAR	No fair? What's that got to do with anything. Do we have to carry her on our backs?
AMBER	I'm healthy and Petra isn't.
OSCAR	So?
AMBER	So? Isn't there room to manoeuvre?
OSCAR	There is so much money for so much work.

AMBER	Why can't it just go on the way it has? I do some design, there's hardly any left, Petra does contract work, there's hardly any left, and… we just…
OSCAR	It's hopeless.
AMBER	Couldn't you just hang on for a while?
OSCAR	I can't do it.
AMBER	What if you weren't alone?
OSCAR	If I wasn't alone?
AMBER	If you weren't carrying it all alone?
OSCAR	How did we become nice people?
AMBER	I don't know.

They kiss.

sleeping with chris

PETRA	You are attracted to me, aren't you? You're attracted to sick people anyway, you're a doctor, you like the feeling of power.
DIANE	I consider myself basically heterosexual.
PETRA	It's got to do with whether or not you're attracted to whatever it is I have. Whether he owns you, whether he has taken over you too.
DIANE	I don't think of illness as possession. No, that's not true, I do.
PETRA	You say you've crossed all the boundaries, but you're really incredibly conventional, you're still on the other side of the line.
DIANE	I don't think so.
PETRA	Emotions are little blind beasts you let out into the night. They don't happily trot themselves out and behave well while we examine them.

DIANE	No, you're actually quite wrong. I have passed the boundaries of convention.
PETRA	You have to deal with me, you have to want me.
DIANE	Thank you, I have a very full sexual life.
PETRA	Liar. Liar, liar pants on fire. You're a dinner alone in front of the TV girl if I ever saw one.
DIANE	Actually not.
PETRA	I want you to blush when I come into the room. I want you to cry when I cry. If you felt what I feel you would know how to make me better. Love me. / Fuck the distance! Fuck professional distance!
DIANE	Don't give me professional distance. I am way, way on the other side of professional distance.
PETRA	I think you're having a nervous breakdown. Is that it? Is it the virus? Is it whispering to you at night? It whispers to me.
DIANE	Something whispers to me at night. I don't think it's a virus.
PETRA	You have to be on the line too.
DIANE	I have lost my distance with you and I don't know why. You're not all that charming, you're not even an extreme case, I have patients so tired they can't lift their arms. So why?
PETRA	You spend all your time pretending there's an answer, a cause. So go all the way. Attach yourself to me, see with my eyes, find a way out.
DIANE	I think I have tried to do that by sleeping with Chris.
PETRA	You slept with Chris?
DIANE	More than once. Now, is that something that breaks the pattern of a one-sided relationship with your doctor?
PETRA	I have to go now. I have to get out of here.
	Are you disappointed? This is your big moment and I don't even care. I don't care because he stayed and he doesn't

even love me. Bastard. You lay around and talked about me. Is that part of your research? Is it love? I could make one phone call, and you would be in so much trouble. This is fun. I want better remedies than this. There's always something new coming out. You find the best stuff and give it to me for free. You love the part of me that's going to go hope, home now and not tell him I know. I still am the core relationship. And maybe it wasn't you that wanted to kiss me, maybe it was me that wanted to kiss you. I find you very attractive. Now run, run as fast as you can go.

the soul

CHRIS   There was a while there, when you just started to lie in bed with your eyes open. I wanted to crawl right inside you. Where are you going? Where's your portal and what's it to? Never in my life has anybody asked me for so much without asking me. I just had to give and as I started to give I started to love you, really love you. And I started to love you at the same time as I was sleeping with Diane. These things exist, these triangles exist in the world and more. By the time I'm totally capable of loving you, you're completely incapable of loving me.

PETRA   I'm not completely incapable. I'm not completely incapable of loving you.

CHRIS   I think we should live together.

PETRA   Because you fucked my doctor?

CHRIS   The last time I was here I dreamt I was flying down my old street on my bike, really fast, just one fantastic kid ego yelling "I'm going fast." I was thinking about how I was going to solve world hunger, bomb everybody, save everybody. I saw people standing by the side of the road and I knew how to help them. If you want me to move in, I'll move in.

PETRA   Because you had a dream?

CHRIS	Because if you're not going to Diane anymore, something big has to change.
PETRA	Who says I'm not going to her any more?
CHRIS	You'd go back to her?
PETRA	No.
CHRIS	I had a bizarre thought that if I slept with her, and then slept with you, you'd get better.
PETRA	But that's not why you did it.
CHRIS	No.
PETRA	And now she's gone. She was the only thing holding me together.
CHRIS	I'm twelve years old, riding down the street with no hands. My heart is so big it's bursting out of me, it's like the sun. I'll heal you.
PETRA	I'm afraid of infecting you.
CHRIS	All this time you've been afraid of us infecting you.
PETRA	Diane wants us to go back for one more session.
CHRIS	No way.

martoonie

DIANE	I turned myself into the medical association, and I'm suspended for two years. I'm free. I'm going to find somewhere that people are healthy, but before I go, I wanted to offer one last session. Close your eyes. Ten. This forest is treacherous, but you can't wait to enter. Nine, as you walk, you come to a glass building. Eight, you see a huge rock, covered with ancient carvings. Seven, at first you're disappointed, the pictures mean nothing. Six, where you saw maybe a dozen petroglyphs, now you see hundreds, thousands. Five, the rock is alive with carvings. There is a face with a mouth wide open. Four, you see strange animals in the rock, trapped, struggling to get out. Three, at the

centre of the rock is a woman, her legs stretch out deep into a fissure. Two, a shaft of light hits her in the belly. One.

DIANE snaps her fingers.

PETRA What?

DIANE Five-thirty. It's martoonie time. I have everything.

CHRIS We're going to have martinis?

DIANE Yes.

DIANE begins mixing.

CHRIS Now?

DIANE It's five-thirty.

CHRIS Why?

PETRA I don't like martinis.

DIANE I even have a shaker.

CHRIS The sound of the shaker feels like coming home, sinking into a chair, and knowing it's all over 'til tomorrow.

DIANE I love the shape of the glass, like an open flower in your hand.

CHRIS I've done acid, but I have to say, gin and vermouth…

DIANE Chin chin. Down the hatch.

CHRIS You want me to chug it?

DIANE You're a brave man. That's good. How's the company doing?

CHRIS Technologies looking a little soft but nothing to worry about.

DIANE There are always market fluctuations. Another one?

CHRIS Sure.

PETRA Don't have the second martini. I know what you're doing. You're trying to press my buttons and it won't work.

CHRIS Petra, you've got to give up your martini phobia.

DIANE Just this once, try it.

PETRA	*(drinks)* No big deal.
DIANE	You haven't had alcohol in a while so it might really affect you.
PETRA	Jesus. My parents were doing this every night?
DIANE	Every night.
PETRA	Wow. Things are looking very old Technicolor. Very bright.
DIANE	See? Nothing wrong with that.
CHRIS	Very bright.
PETRA	And I'm happy, so happy. I think it's great you two got together, no I mean it. It makes me feel loved. You two love each other and you love me and that's the way it should be. We should all have a child.
CHRIS	A child would be good.
DIANE	A lot can happen when folks are sick. No, delete that. I'm from Cape Breton and they don't say folks there, even though people think they do. They say, "people" or "everybody," but nothing like "folks." I don't think anybody says it, I think it comes from telesision. Hi, "folks." It's so irritating.
CHRIS	Telesision? Is that the second martini talking?
DIANE	Television. Series television.
CHRIS	Diane, I don't want you to take this badly, but you're starting to slur your words.
DIANE	What do you mean? When? Just now?
CHRIS	Just now.
DIANE	No it's not. I'm perfectly comprehensible.
CHRIS	And your eyes are starting to droop. Look, there. Droopy, droopy eyes.
DIANE	Don't be ridulous.
CHRIS	Ridiculous? You can't take two, just admit it. Maybe you should just lie down.
DIANE	I'm not slurring my words. And I don't want to lie down.

CHRIS	Just take it easy. Feeling a little dizzy? Next time, just have one, there's a good girl.
DIANE	Don't be silly.
CHRIS	Maybe it's the cocktails that're making you put on all that weight. Look at your stomach, you're getting that menopausal pear shape. Folds of loose flesh hanging over your pants…
VIRUS	For some reason the mother could only imagine passive resistance. So she went to the store, and with her housekeeping money, she bought her own bottle of vodka, her own vermouth, her own jar of olives and she hid the bottles in the pockets of her old fur coat in the hall cupboard. Just before the father came home, the mother would mix herself a stiff one and drink it all alone, hiding.
DIANE	I can't lose the weight, I've been eating nothing.
CHRIS	If you cut down on the martinis, you'll lose all that flab.
DIANE	I'm not cutting down on the martoonies…
CHRIS	You see?
DIANE	I'm not a heavy drinker, I just like a drink / at the…
CHRIS	/ Who were you calling today? I tried to call twice and the phone was busy. Who were you talking to?
DIANE	I was calling my sister.
CHRIS	Why? You're spending all afternoon on the phone, / talking to…
DIANE	/ I wasn't on all day.
CHRIS	I called twice. Why were you on the phone?
DIANE	I have to call her sometime.
CHRIS	You've spilled something down your front.
DIANE	No, I haven't.
CHRIS	It's dripping.
DIANE	It's just dripping…

CHRIS	I'm going to have to make a mark on the bottle, see how much is gone.
DIANE	Mark the bottles?
CHRIS	You can't handle two.
DIANE	I can. I can, it's just that you're making me / nervous
CHRIS	/ You're slurring your words.
DIANE	I'm not slurring my words.
CHRIS	You're eyes are drooping, look your face has gone all red.
DIANE	Stop it. You're giving me a headache.
CHRIS	Your eyes are halfway open. Just go to bed, there's a good girl
DIANE	I'm not going to bed.
CHRIS	You've got a headache.
DIANE	That doesn't bean, mean I / have to…
CHRIS	You're a sickie. Go to bed.
DIANE	Don't call me that.
CHRIS	You're a sickie, go to bed.
DIANE	Stop it.
CHRIS	You can't handle two. You can't keep up.
DIANE	You're giving me a headache.
CHRIS	You were probably in bed all day. A sickie again.
DIANE	No, I wasn't.
CHRIS	She's a sickie again.
DIANE	Don't call me a sickie. You're making me sick.
CHRIS	Yes, she's a sickie. Just go to bed now, where you've been all day. Sickie.
DIANE	Stop that.
CHRIS	Sickie.
DIANE	Now I have to go to bed, my head is cracking…

PETRA   Noooooooooooooooooooooooooooo

               PETRA screams.

CHRIS   Oh God.

DIANE   Petra, there's nothing more I, or anyone else can do for you. Some people get better after five years, no one knows why. But if you pass the five year mark and are still symptomatic, all indications are that you'll be like this for the rest of your life. I believe what just happened will help, although I can't say in what way.

              `white light`

VIRUS   You dance divinely.

PETRA   Yes, I know.

VIRUS   Are you ready to accept me?

PETRA   Good people are dead. Good people are sick. I am not okay with it. I do not accept. I am outraged that this has happened to me. I am outraged that illness, poverty, war, disease, natural catastrophes happen. I am outraged over whether or not I have a right to protest my poor little version of evil. I'm outraged that there's anything worse than what I have to compare myself to.

VIRUS   Absolutely. That's a good move.

PETRA   Did you see how I did that? It's an undulation, very big now, they're all big on undulations. They come from the reptilian brain.

VIRUS   You were saying about acceptance…

PETRA   All this time I've been fighting for someone to say it's real, and now she's said it…

VIRUS   Now you're outraged. That's good.

PETRA   Now I don't want to admit you exist. I love this music. Did you see how I did that? And even as I say it, I don't believe it. Even though I believe that one brush against you would make me sleep forever. Even though I believe that one solid dose of happiness would be your undoing.

VIRUS   I think it's admirable you're outraged about the world, even about your friends. It won't be long before they get it too. Union, transcription, replication, assembly, release.

PETRA   I thought I could do battle with you and that was wrong. I thought I could be smarter than you and that was wrong. I thought I could manipulate myself into transcendence and that was wrong. I think maybe I should love you, but I can't. So I have just one question. What's your name?

VIRUS   No.

PETRA   What's your name?

VIRUS   It won't help you.

PETRA   Maybe not. But there's a lot in a name. Come on, give. If you tell me your name, I'll kiss you.

VIRUS   Kiss me? You'll kiss me, not I kiss you?

PETRA   Yes.

VIRUS   You kiss me?

PETRA   Yes.

VIRUS   It's an offer. Only one little kiss? Not two? Two and some smooching?

PETRA   One. Come closer.

VIRUS   You can't kill me.

PETRA   I know. Union, transcription, replication, assembly, release.

PETRA kisses the VIRUS.

The VIRUS whispers in her ear.

PETRA turns to the audience. As she speaks, CHRIS, DIANE, OSCAR and AMBER curl up and sleep.

How are you feeling? One. Nothing has harmed you, nothing will invade your home tonight. Two. Your thoughts are filled with forests so green it breaks your heart. Three. There may be darkness there, don't be afraid. Four. You sense a soft wateriness flooding your mouth. Five. You hear the murmur of an old language spoken deep in your belly. Six. A curtain of grey falls from your eyes, leaving them clear as a forest pool. Seven. The tension in your shoulders and neck is melting away. Eight. Tune into your breath, as it drops in and falls out effortlessly, it is a tide and a force. Nine. Tonight, when you go home, you'll sleep deeper than you've slept since you were twelve years old. Perverse and innocent. A deep healing sleep. Ten.

Curtain.

The end.

photo by Susan King

As playwright and actor, Griffiths is the winner of five Dora Mavor Moore Awards, a Gemini award, two Chalmer's awards, the Quizanne International Festival Award for *Jessica*, and Los Angeles' A.G.A. Award for her title performance in the John Sayles' film "Lianna." She has twice been nominated for the Governor General's Award (*The Darling Family*, *Alien Creature*). Her nine plays include *Chronic, Alien Creature, The Duchess: a.k.a Wallis Simpson* and *Maggie & Pierre*. She is the co-author of a unique theatre book – *The Book of Jessica* (co-written with Native author and activist Maria Campbell). Griffiths has created collective work (*Paper Wheat, Les Maudits Anglais*), and published short stories ("The Speed Christmas," "Spiral Woman"). Her company, Duchess Productions develops and helps to produce her work, including a new invention – a playwrighting class called Visceral Playwrighting. A partial anthology, *Sheer Nerve: Seven Plays by Linda Griffiths* is available through Playwrights Canada Press. Her next play is based on the Victorian novel by George Gissing, *The Odd Women*.